TABLE OF CONTENTS

Unless otherwise indicated, all Scripture quotations are taken from the King James Version of the Bible.
7 Rewards of Problem-Solving, Seeds of Wisdom on Problem-Solving, Vol. 16
ISBN 1-56394-112-0/B-118
Copyright © 2001 by **MIKE MURDOCK**
All publishing rights belong exclusively to Wisdom International
Published by The Wisdom Center · 4051 Denton Hwy. · Ft. Worth, Texas 76117
1-817-759-BOOK · 1-817-759-0300
You Will Love Our Website...! TheWisdomCenter.tv

You Will Only
Be Pursued
For The Problems
You Can Solve.

-MIKE MURDOCK

❧ 1 ❧

You Were Created To Solve A Problem On Earth

You Contain Solutions.

Everything created is a solution to a specific problem on the earth. Your eyes see. Your ears hear. Your mind thinks. Your mouth speaks. It is so important to understand this.

Mechanics solve car problems. Mothers solve emotional problems. Dentists solve teeth problems. Lawyers solve legal problems. Ministers solve spiritual problems. The problem you were created to solve is your personal Assignment on the earth. This Assignment is the key to your joy and reward. "To rejoice in his labor; this is the gift of God," (Ecclesiastes 5:19).

Now, you are not designed nor assigned to solve every problem for everyone. This is as important as knowing the problem you are assigned to solve. Jesus knew this. That's why He explained to the Pharisees that He was called to those who recognized their insufficiency and need of Him. He never invested time in those who erroneously thought they were whole.

4 Keys To Recognizing The Problem You Were Created To Solve

1.   **The Problem That Infuriates You The**

Most Is Often The Problem God Has Assigned You To Solve. Anger is passion. Anger is energy requiring an appropriate focus. Anger is always a necessary ingredient for uncommon change.

What angers you is a clue to an existing problem God intends for you to solve. It is a signal from God to correct something that grieves Him.

Anger is often a signpost in your life. It is the birthplace for *change*. The Scriptures provide an excellent example. When Moses observed an Egyptian beating up an Israelite, his anger rose. Why? He was a Deliverer of the Israelites. True, his reaction to the Egyptian was wrong, but it was a photograph of his passion. Give attention to those problems that unleash fury, anger and a holy passion within you. Perhaps it is child abuse, battered wives, drug addiction or alcoholism. Whatever it is that stirs your passion for change, is a signal in your life.

Some years ago, a mother saw her child lying dead on the pavement because of a drunk driver. Her anger was so strong, she launched a powerful and significant organization to stop people from drinking while driving.

Those angered by *injustice* often become lawyers. Those angered by *disease* often become doctors. Those angered by *poverty* unleash motivation courses on excellence and productivity.

2. What You Love The Most Is A Clue To The Problem You Are Gifted To Solve. Do you love computers? That's where your Wisdom will be. Do you love children? You probably possess an innate and intuitive ability to communicate and aid children.

The Proof Of Love Is The Investment Of Time.

Whatever you are willing to spend time on is a clue to something you value.

3. What Grieves Your Heart Continually Is A Clue To A Problem God Wants You To Solve. When you see television programs that make you weep for starving children, that is a clue to a problem God is linking you to.

4. Your Dominant Gift Is Often A Clue To The Problem You Were Created To Solve. Are you gifted with numbers? Work with children? Administration and organization? Music? Your gift is the bridge to the problem you were created to solve.

Remember: *You Were Created To Solve A Specific Problem On Earth.*

The Problem You Are
Willing To Solve
Determines Who
Pursues You.

-MIKE MURDOCK

2

PROBLEMS ARE THE BIRTHPLACE FOR UNCOMMON PROMOTIONS AND NEW RELATIONSHIPS

Problems Are Golden Keys To Change.

When Pharaoh faced depression, Joseph entered. When King Saul was tormented by evil spirits, David entered. When his countrymen faced annihilation, Jephthah reentered.

Any problem you are experiencing contains a gold mine of Wisdom, opportunity and potential promotion. It is your responsibility to discern it.

1. Problems Birth New Relationships. David married the daughter of the king...by solving the problem of Goliath. The unwatered camels of the servant of Abraham...became the Golden Link for Rebekah to meet and marry Isaac. The famine activated Naomi's move to Bethlehem. There, Ruth met Boaz. Nabal cursed David, refusing to provide food for his men, it was the Golden Bridge connecting Abigail and David.

2. Problems Are Gates To Change. Pharaoh gave the position of Prime Minister to Joseph *after* he solved the unexplained dream.

When Haman threatened to annihilate the Jews,

that problem made Esther willing to expose Haman's heart to the king. So, Haman lost his position of influence with the king.

3. Problems Are The Keys To Recognition And Promotion. When the king experienced great anger and depression over a forgotten dream, it was Daniel's corridor for promotion.

Always look at a problem as the camouflage for significance and promotion. Problems are glorious Seeds that grow into Golden Harvests.

4. Every Problem You Are Facing Must Be Identified And Clearly Defined. You can only solve a problem you can define. It is often hidden.

5. Something You Possess Will Solve Any Problem You Face. David had the slingshot to kill Goliath. Moses had the rod to part the sea. The widow of Zarephath had one last pancake to begin her Harvest. Inventory your personal passion, potential and skills. *Always Inventory What You Have Received From God.* It may be simply the gift of access to an uncommon leader, a good name created by trustworthy parents, or your tenacity to finish what you begin.

So, don't run from a problem. Search for the hidden gold within it. In the ashes of every failure lie Diamonds of Discovery and gold worth a fortune.

Remember: *Problems Are The Birthplace For Uncommon Promotions And New Relationships.*

≈ 3 ≈

The Problem Nearest You Is Usually Your Secret Door Out Of Trouble

Everybody Has Problems.

The poor despise their poverty and fear total loss. The wealthy fear theft and potential loss of position and respect.

Some are open and free to discuss their problems with anybody and everyone. Others, discreet or secretive, seek to hide their pain and torment from friends. But, everybody has problems.

5 Important Keys To Remember When You Face A Problem

1. Jesus Is Our Example As The Master Problem-Solver. "I am the vine, ye are the branches: he that abideth in Me, and I in him, the same bringeth forth much fruit: for without Me ye can do nothing," (John 15:5).

2. God Is Always Aware Of Every Problem You Are Facing. He promised that He would not permit any problem too great for us to handle.

David understood this all-knowing God. "Thou knowest my downsitting and mine uprising, Thou understandest my thought afar off...and art acquainted with all my ways...Thou hast beset me behind and before, and laid Thine hand upon me," (Psalm 139:2-5).

3. God Has Qualified You To Solve The Problem Nearest You...For A Reason. When Joseph noticed the downcast countenances of the butler and the baker under his care in prison, he responded. He questioned them. His compassion emerged. He moved swiftly to interpret their dreams. He remembered to give God the glory. You see, it was the plan of God.

Joseph *noticed* the problem.

Joseph *cared* about the problem being solved.

Joseph was *capable* of solving the problem. "Withhold not good from them to whom it is due, when it is in the power of thine hand to do it," (Proverbs 3:27).

David solved the problem closest to him. When he heard the cursing of Goliath, anger erupted. He saw the fear on the faces of his brothers and soldiers. His confidence in God, his memory of defeating the lion and the bear was strong within him. His imagination burst with the photograph that he could kill Goliath.

It was the problem closest to him...that became his Door into significance and favor.

Rewards were unleashed upon him. He became debt-free. He did not have to pay taxes any more. He married the king's daughter. The favor of Israel flowed over his life like Niagara Falls. Goliath was simply the problem closest to him.

Ruth solved the problem closest to her. Naomi was embittered. Distraught, Naomi explained to Ruth that she had no more sons for Ruth to marry. Her husband was dead. Her sons were dead. She had nothing. But, Ruth solved her problem of loneliness and tragedy. "Intreat me not to leave thee, or to return from following after thee: for whither thou goest, I will go; and where thou lodgest, I will lodge: thy people shall be my people, and thy God my God," (Ruth 1:16). It was her Golden Connection to the Boaz of her lifetime.

4. The Problem Closest To You May Appear Simple But May Produce Incredible Rewards. Remember the miraculous story of Rebekah? The chief servant of Abraham was weary and tired. As he ended his journey that day...his camels were thirsty. The long caravan would take many hours to water. But, Rebekah saw the problem. She saw the fatigue. It mattered to her. She offered to help water those camels. Watering those camels transferred the wealth of Abraham into her life.

The simplest problem is often the Golden Gate hiding your greatest rewards.

It is the problem nearest you and your attitude toward solving it...that unlocks The Blessing.

5. When You Solve A Problem For Others, You Schedule A Divine Solution To A Problem In Your Own Future. "Knowing that whatsoever good thing any man doeth, the same shall he receive of the Lord, whether he be bond or free," (Ephesians 6:8).

Remember: *The Problem Nearest You Is Usually Your Secret Door Out Of Trouble.*

The Problems You Solve
Determine
The Rewards You Receive.

-MIKE MURDOCK

❧ 4 ❧

YOUR REWARDS IN LIFE ARE DETERMINED BY THE KINDS OF PROBLEMS YOU ARE WILLING TO SOLVE FOR OTHERS

◄══════►▶◄○◄══════►

Your Salary Depends On The Problem You Solve.

12 Rewards Problem-Solvers Receive

1.   The Problem You Solve Can Generate Credibility With Others.   When the Apostle Paul helped bring the healing power of God to the father Publius, the chief of the island, favor flowed.   Others were healed. The physician Luke documents, "Who also honoured us with many honours; and when we departed, they laded us with such things as were necessary," (Acts 28:10).   The same people who were suspicious that Paul was evil, changed their mind completely *after he solved a problem* for their leader!

2.   The Problem You Solve May Schedule An Eventual Reward Years In Your Future. Mordecai experienced this. Years after he exposed the assassination attempt on the king, he was rewarded. One night, the king could not sleep.   So, he read the various events that had happened in the past. As he reviewed his journal, it dawned on him that Mordecai had never been compensated for exposing the strategy to destroy him. So, he had Haman, the chief adversary of Mordecai, parade Mordecai through the streets... shouting to everyone that the king was honoring this man. Years prior, Mordecai had *solved a problem.*

3. The Problem You Solve Can Cause Others To Celebrate You. It happened in the life of young David. Though just a shepherd boy, he visited his brothers who were in battle. He was bringing them their lunch as his father had instructed him. Goliath was cursing Israel. David defeated Goliath with a single stone. Within hours, the women of Israel were singing, "Saul has slain his thousands, but David his ten thousands!" The problem he had solved caused great celebration of his life.

4. The Problem You Solve Determines Your Salary. Attorneys receive $200 an hour. Garbage collectors may receive $15. Why? Two kinds of problems. Your salary does not reflect your personal worth, gifts or capabilities. Your salary is simply decided by the kind of problem you have chosen to solve for your boss.

If there are many people capable of solving the specific problem you presently solve for your boss, your salary will be less. You could be easily replaced. If you alone can solve that specific problem, your salary is increased. (Few can match your skills!)

5. The Problem You Solve Determines How You Will Be Remembered. King Saul offered a huge reward for killing Goliath. David pursued knowledge of the rewards when he heard the cursing of Goliath. He was told, "The king will enrich him with great riches, and will give him his daughter, and make his father's house free in Israel," (1 Samuel 17:25).

6. The Problem You Solve Determines Your Eternal Rewards From God. Continually, God promises to reward us according to our works. "For the Son of man shall come in the glory of His Father with His angels; and then He shall *reward every man according to his works,*" (Matthew 16:27).

The Kingdom of God thrives on *The Reward System.* John, in Revelation, continuously reports the special gifts, promotions and recognition that will be provided to those who overcome (see Revelation 2:3).

7. The Problem You Solve May Position You For Friendship With Uncommon Leaders. When David experienced his victory over Goliath, the heart of Jonathan, the son of the king, was knitted with David. When Joseph solved the problem for Pharaoh and his dream, Pharaoh instantly made him second in command.

8. The Problem You Solve Causes Uncommon People To See Your Distinction From Others. It happened when Ruth became a provider for Naomi. The wealthy landowner, Boaz, recognized her. When Daniel provided the interpretation for the king, he was immediately promoted and recognized.

9. The Problem You Solve Can Unleash An Increase Of The Blessings Of God. "The Lord shall open unto thee His good treasure, the heaven to give the rain unto thy land in His season, and to bless all the work of thine hand," (Deuteronomy 28:12).

10. The Problem You Solve Will Determine The Quality Of Leaders Who Pursue You. "Seest thou a man diligent in his business? he shall stand before kings," (Proverbs 22:29).

11. The Problem You Solve Can Cause You To Become The Topic Of Discussion Among Others Who Face Similar Problems. Boaz knew that Ruth treated Naomi better than seven sons would treat their mother. Daniel was recommended to the king. The butler *remembered* Joseph two years later after his dream was interpreted by Joseph. He commended Joseph to Pharaoh. Joseph became Prime Minister.

12. The Problem You Solve Is Your Difference From Others. Without a problem, relationships cannot exist. Without a problem, your gift can remain dormant for years. The brothers of David sneered at him. In fact, they were quite angry at him. But, Goliath was his Bridge to Recognition.

Your telephone will never ring unless someone has a problem they want you to solve. It may be emotional, reassurance, specific information or simply a question that needs answering.

Several years ago, a new secretary buzzed my office.

"Dr. Mike, the young couple who was scheduled to bring you to the airport tomorrow, has decided to go shopping instead. Could you drive yourself to the airport tomorrow?"

I was flabbergasted. Great frustration rose up in me. Here I was, traveling around the world, carrying luggage and sleeping in strange hotel rooms...and they wanted to go shopping instead of making a 25 minute drive to the airport.

I remembered that a lady on my staff had always asked me to let her know if there was any problem she could solve. She had four teenage children so, I was always reluctant to involve her in projects. Her hands were full, I knew. But, I decided to make the suggestion to her. She was so cooperative.

"Oh, Dr. Murdock, it would be a delight and an honor to assist you."

Several weeks later, I explained to her that my flight from California would arrive at 5:50 a.m., much too early for her to make the drive to pick me up.

"I will just take the taxi," I explained.

"Oh, no! I would not dream of a man of God having to sit in the back of a taxi! I will be there on schedule." She was adamant about it. Sure enough, when I arrived from the all-night flight, she was there, smiling and happy. In fact, she had even purchased herself a chauffeur's uniform, with a chauffeur's hat! She never complained one time about the burden of rescheduling her time with her children, other projects and so forth.

She was dependable. Trustworthy. Faithful. And, enthusiastic about removing that burden from me. A few weeks later, someone handed me $200 as I walked out of a service and said, "Do anything you want with this $200."

When I landed at the airport, I remembered that school was starting for her four children.

I handed her the $200.

"Somebody gave me $200...and I know you need school supplies for your children. Here, buy them some school supplies today."

Later, someone gave me $500 and said, "Give it to anyone you want or whatever you want to do with it." I thought of this diligent young lady when I arrived at the airport that day.

I handed the $500 to her and said, "I know how desperately you need some clothes. Here go buy yourself some clothes. Somebody gave this to me." When her car broke down, it was a joy to make an investment and help her purchase a good car. She was a passionate *Problem-Solver.*

5 Simple Steps That May Increase Your Income Within 90 Days!

1.   Change The Kind Of Problems You Are Solving For Your Company. Every problem has a different monetary value.

2.   Change Your Attitude And Accuracy With Which You Solve The Problems. Excellence is always the difference in employees.

3.   Change The Company You Are Solving The Problems For. God's plan often involves geographical changes (see Ruth 1-4).

4.   Ask Your boss To Correct Any Behavior In You That Agitates Him. Those who embrace correction easily always receive the Gift of Access to leaders.

5.   Become A True Protegé Of Your Supervisor, Pursuing His Counsel And Standard Of Excellence.

Remember: *Your Rewards In Life Are Determined By The Kinds Of Problems You Are Willing To Solve For Others.*

RECOMMENDED FOR YOUR WISDOM LIBRARY:
B-01 Wisdom for Winning (228 pages/$10)
B-40 Wisdom for Crisis Times (112 pages/$9)
B-91 The Leadership Secrets of Jesus (196 pages/$10)

⚜ 5 ⚜

WHEN YOU DETERMINE TO BE AN UNCOMMON PROBLEM-SOLVER, YOU WILL UNLEASH UNCOMMON FAVOR

Problems Are Gates To Favor.

When You Solve An Uncommon Problem, You Will Change The Attitude Of Others Toward You. Remember my earlier reference to Paul, shipwrecked on the island? As he gathered sticks to build a fire, a snake attached itself to his arm. Those observing thought he must "be evil." When Paul calmly shook off the snake in the fire and continued without harm, their attitude changed. They thought he was a god. Luke recorded that they overwhelmed Paul and him with gifts upon their departure.

When You Become An Uncommon Problem-Solver, You Will Instantly Gain Access To Uncommon Leaders And Champions. Pharaoh gave Joseph instant access to the treasures of Egypt...within 24 hours. Why? He solved a problem *nobody* else could solve. When You Solve A Problem For Someone In The Palace, They Become Your Exit From Prison.

6 Keys To Becoming An Uncommon Problem-Solver

1.   Solve A Problem Quickly And Swiftly. *Diligence is immediate attention to an assigned task.* Any boss views an employee who slows him down as adversarial. "Seest thou a man diligent in his business? he shall stand before kings," (Proverbs 22:29).

2.   Solve Problems Cheerfully. In my book, *Secrets of the Richest Man Who Ever Lived,* I share one of the remarkable secrets of Solomon, who built a $500 billion temple. He only hired happy people. "Righteous lips are the delight of kings; and they love him that speaketh right," (Proverbs 16:13).

3.   Solve A Problem Others Refuse To Correct. The story of Naaman, the leper general of Syria, is fascinating. Leprosy always alienated families and communities. It is a disease that can remain hidden for years. But, his handmaiden decided to link him with the prophet, Elisha. It was her *difference.*

4.   Solve A Problem Others Are Incapable Of Solving. David killed Goliath, when others were fearful of him. Joseph interpreted a dream nobody else understood.

5.   Solve A Problem For Someone Too Tired And Weary To Solve It. It was the secret of Rebekah. She became the wife of Isaac and heir to the wealth of Abraham. She was compassionate toward an old man!

6.   Solve The Most Difficult Problem To Become Qualified For The Greatest Rewards. King Saul explained this when he offered a tax-free lifestyle to any warrior who would defeat Goliath. Goliath was not a common enemy. He was over nine feet tall. His voice struck fear in the heart of every Israelite soldier. Goliath was an *uncommon* problem. So, the reward that was offered for killing him was also uncommon. *The Size Of Your Enemy Determines The Size Of Your Reward.*

6 Facts Every Problem-Solver Should Remember

1. An Uncommon Problem Will Often Require Uncommon Prayer And Intercession. Esther did not trust her beauty to solidify her favor with the king. She personally fasted. She called others to fast. True, she was the most beautiful woman in 127 provinces from India to Ethiopia. But, she knew that the problem with Haman was not common. She needed a miracle. She needed *uncommon* favor. She needed *uncommon* Wisdom. So, she was willing to pay an *uncommon* price—fasting and prayer.

2. An Uncommon Problem-Solver Is Always Pursued By Uncommon Leaders. That is why the king loved discussing Elisha, with the *servant* of Elisha, Gehazi. They discussed the incredible miracles even in the palace, without the presence of Elisha. Throughout history, those willing to solve difficult problems are often praised, recognized and even publicly rewarded by leaders. In the medical field, those who find the vaccine that destroys dreaded diseases...*become celebrated.*

3. The Solution Is Often Much Simpler Than The Problem Appears. Nothing Is Ever As

Difficult As It First Appears. It simply awaits those who *persist*.

4. The Holy Spirit Has Often Qualified You To Solve The Very Problem You Recognize. *Recognizing* a problem is often a clue that *you* contain the gift to solve it!

5. Quality Time Invested In The Secret Place Will Often Reveal The Divine Design For Solving The Problem. The Holy Spirit is our Advisor. *Never attempt to fight an earthly battle without heavenly weaponry.*

6. Some Problems Will Require The Supernatural Counsel And Empowering Of The Holy Spirit To Solve. Avoid the arrogance of self-sufficiency. "Lean not unto thine own understanding," (Proverbs 3:5). Prayerlessness is arrogance.

Remember: *When You Determine To Be An Uncommon Problem-Solver, You Will Unleash Uncommon Favor.*

❦ **6** ❦

YOU WILL ONLY BE REMEMBERED IN LIFE FOR TWO THINGS—THE PROBLEMS YOU SOLVE OR THE ONES YOU CREATE

———▸❖◂———

Problems Are Keys To Your Legacy.

Every friendship is formed because of the problem it solves. Problems are the only reason people stay friends. When mates cease to solve problems for each other, they *become* a problem to each other.

Many of us are familiar with the names of Adolph Hitler, Stalin, Mussolini and Charles Manson, the killer. They are remembered by millions...because of the problems they created.

You will be remembered...by someone.

You may be remembered as a Problem. You may be remembered as a Solution.

Goliath is remembered as The Problem.

David is remembered as The Solution.

Haman is remembered for the problem he created...the conspiracy against the Jews. While Esther is remembered as the queen who saved the Jews. She was a Problem-Solver.

6 Keys To Establishing Your Legacy As A Problem-Solver

1. Do Not Try To Solve Problems For Everyone. Perhaps you are not a dentist or a plumber or a mechanic. It is important that you not take the responsibility for problems you cannot solve.

2. Decide What Problem You Want To Be Remembered For Solving. Many great medical researchers have focused on finding the cure...for one specific disease. It's the way they want to be remembered.

3. Do Not Attempt To Solve Too Many Problems At The Same Time. J. Paul Getty, the billionaire, said that he had seen as many people fail from attempting too many things as attempting too few.

4. Always Solve Problems Cheerfully. It increases favor. "A merry heart doeth good like a medicine," (Proverbs 17:22).

5. Become Detail Conscious And Solve Problems Accurately Without Supervision. "The hand of the diligent shall bear rule," (Proverbs 12:23). Those with the *highest* level of Excellence always become the leaders in any organization.

6. Remember That Problems Are Opportunities To Reveal Your Distinction From Others. Joseph is remembered because he *solved* the problem of provision during famine. Ruth is remembered for *solving* the problems of Naomi. Daniel is remembered for *solving* the problem of the unexplained dream. Absalom is remembered for creating problems with his rebellion to David.

Remember: *You Will Only Be Remembered In Life For Two Things—The Problems You Solve Or The Ones You Create.*

7

Any Uncommon Problem-Solver In Your Life Deserves Your Honor And Recognition

Problem-Solvers Should Always Be Rewarded.

Think for a moment. You have succeeded today because someone solved problems for you throughout your lifetime.

Your Parents Were The First Problem-Solvers In Your Life. They taught you how to eat, how to walk. They insisted upon you learning in school. When you rebelled, they provided the gift of discipline. When you made mistakes, they forgave. Parents are the key Problem-Solvers in most families.

The first commandment with a promise was: "Honour thy father and thy mother: that thy days may be long upon the land which the Lord thy God giveth thee," (Exodus 20:12).

As I write this chapter, it is Memorial Day. I spent the entire afternoon with my father. We had lunch together, and drove around observing various parks and lakes here in Dallas. I would not dream of my father buying anything for me. He has already invested his whole life in me. *Now, it's my turn!* That's why I purchased his car, his home and try to plant generous Seeds into his life at every possible opportunity. Why?

He gave me life! He introduced me to Jesus!

Your pastor is an Uncommon Problem-Solver in your life. He ignites your passion for God. He keeps you warned, corrected and encouraged. He deserves recognition.

Your boss is an Uncommon Problem-Solver in your life. Your boss recognized your gift, and then wrote you a check for using your skills and gifts. Your boss is a Golden Key to your financial foundation. He deserves recognition and reward.

Those who unlock your faith are Problem-Solvers. Years ago, a great missionary evangelist unlocked my Seed-sowing into the work of God. As he told the illustrations of God multiplying Seed back to us, my faith leaped. I took a bold step of faith to make a faith-promise. Within seven days, the hand of God moved in my life. I started sending him a turkey every Thanksgiving...in honor of how he unlocked my faith.

The person who introduced you to Christ was a major Problem-Solver in your life. Who brought you to Christ? Whose anointing was the magnet that swept you into the presence of Jesus? Who prayed the sinner's prayer over your life? Who prayed the prayer of faith that brought you healing and health?

Your life is surrounded by Problem-Solvers! ...bankers, lawyers and doctors. Never overlook this. Never take it lightly. Whether it is the maid that cleans your house, the mechanic that repairs your car or the cheerful clerk checking your groceries...many are helping you solve the problems in your life. *Recognize them.*

Your Personal Checklist Form Celebrating The Uncommon Problem-Solvers In Your Life

Write the names below of *The Top 10 Problem-Solvers* in your life, past and present.

1._____
2._____
3._____
4._____
5._____
6._____
7._____
8._____
9._____
10._____

Now write down *three things* you can do for them within 30 days to document your gratitude (a phone call, a letter or a gift).

1._____
2._____
3._____

▶ Anything Unrecognized Becomes Uncelebrated.
▶ Anything Uncelebrated Becomes Unrewarded.
▶ Anything Unrewarded Will Exit Your Life.

***What You Make Happen For Others, God Will
Make Happen For You.*** "Knowing that whatsoever
good thing any man doeth, the same shall he receive
of the Lord, whether he be bond or free," (Ephesians
6:8).

Remember: *Any Uncommon Problem-Solver In
Your Life Deserves Your Recognition And Reward.*

Our Prayer Together...

"Heavenly Father, thank You for Jesus Who has
solved my many problems. Thank You for The
Holy Spirit Who provides me with daily
Wisdom for my life. Thank You for The Uncommon
Problem-Solvers around me who have made my life so
much easier.

*Anoint me today to become an Uncommon
Problem-Solver for others around me.* I receive that
anointing in the name of Jesus. Amen."

My Closing Thought

*If this Wisdom Book has blessed you, I'd love to
hear from you!* You may order additional copies for a
friend, cell group, or associates at your workplace.
The Greatest Gift Of All...Is The Gift Of Wisdom.

Quantity Price List For
7 Rewards of Problem-Solving (B-118)

QUANTITY	COST EACH	DISCOUNT	QUANTITY	COST EACH	DISCOUNT
1-9	= $5.00 ea.	Retail	2000-4999	= $2.00 ea.	60%
10-499	= $3.00 ea.	40%	5000-up	= Contact Office	
500-1999	= $2.50 ea.	50%			

(Add 10% shipping single titles only.)

DECISION

Will You Accept Jesus As Your Personal Savior Today?

The Bible says, "That if thou shalt confess with thy mouth the Lord Jesus, and shalt believe in thine heart that God hath raised Him from the dead, thou shalt be saved," (Romans 10:9).

Pray this prayer from your heart today!

"Dear Jesus, I believe that You died for me and rose again on the third day. I confess I am a sinner...I need Your love and forgiveness...Come into my heart. Forgive my sins. I receive Your eternal life. Confirm Your love by giving me peace, joy and supernatural love for others. Amen."

DR. MIKE MURDOCK

is in tremendous demand as one of the most dynamic speakers in America today.

More than 16,000 audiences in 39 countries have attended his conferences and Schools of Wisdom. Hundreds of invitations come to him from churches, colleges and business corporations. He is a noted author of over 200 books, including the best sellers, *The Leadership Secrets of Jesus* and *Secrets of the Richest Man Who Ever Lived.* Thousands view his weekly television program, *Wisdom Keys with Mike Murdock.* Many attend his Schools of Wisdom that he hosts in major cities of America.

Clip and Mail

☐ Yes, Mike! I made a decision to accept Christ as my personal Savior today. Please send me my free gift of your book, *31 Keys to a New Beginning* to help me with my new life in Christ.

NAME   BIRTHDAY

ADDRESS

CITY   STATE   ZIP

PHONE   E-MAIL

Mail form to:

The Wisdom Center · 4051 Denton Hwy. · Ft. Worth, TX 76117
1-817-759-BOOK · 1-817-759-0300
You Will Love Our Website...! TheWisdomCenter.tv   29

JOIN THE

Wisdom Key 3000
TODAY!

Will You Become My Ministry Partner In The Work Of God?

Dear Friend,

God has connected us!

I have asked The Holy Spirit for 3000 Special Partners who will plant a monthly Seed of $58.00 to help me bring the gospel around the world. (58 represents 58 kinds of blessings in the Bible.)

Will you become my monthly Faith Partner in The Wisdom Key 3000? Your monthly Seed of $58.00 is so powerful in helping heal broken lives. When you sow into the work of God, 4 Miracle Harvests are guaranteed in Scripture, Isaiah 58...

- ▸ Uncommon Health (Isaiah 58)
- ▸ Uncommon Wisdom For Decision-Making (Isaiah 58)
- ▸ Uncommon Financial Favor (Isaiah 58)
- ▸ Uncommon Family Restoration (Isaiah 58)

Your Faith Partner,

Mike Murdock

P.S. Please clip the coupon attached and return it to me today, so I can rush the Wisdom Key Partnership Pak to you...or call me at 1-817-759-0300.

Tax Reduction...!

Since God has brought you into my life with a $58 Seed, it has turned my life around. God has changed my heart so much because of your wisdom and your ministry, I never knew God so personally as I am now learning about. I never knew how close to Him I could get and how much He could change things in my life and in me and in other people's lives just by believing that He could. I never knew what taking a step of faith could actually be and what it could do. I'm learning so much about the Lord that I never knew before.

He also took our back taxes from $75,000 to $5,729 from our $58 Seed.

J. & A. M. TN

My Child Can Walk...!

Thought I would write and let you know that my life is making severe changes. Sowing Seed into your ministry has brought about my first set of miracles. I have been sowing Seeds of $58 for over a year and a half to Daystar Television and I know that I have had several breakthroughs because of it. One of the $58 Seeds to the television ministry set a miracle in motion for my daughter...She was 2 1/2 and still not walking. I sowed, prayed and watched. She was in therapy because of her being premature. One of the therapists sat me down and told me she needed leg braces for at least a year and half before she would be able to walk. Within two weeks after their report, after the Seed, after the prayer she began to walk.

C. F. TX

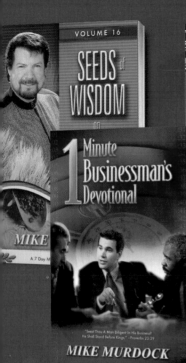
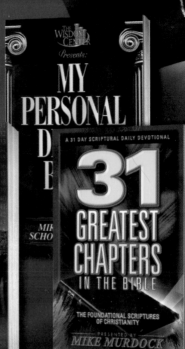

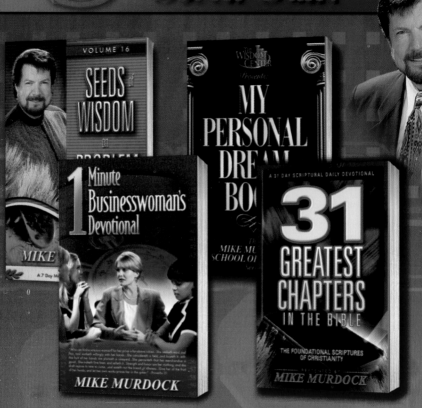

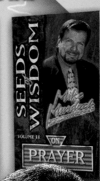
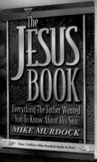
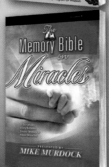

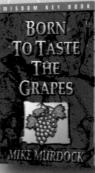

Spirit Music.

The Mike Murdock Music Library

LOVE SONGS TO THE HOLY SPIRIT

Written In The Secret Place

TS-59

DR. MIKE MURDOCK

THE HOLY SPIRIT HANDBOOK

What You Need To Know About Your Daily Companion, The Holy Spirit

MIKE MURDOCK

The Wisdom Center
Free Book ENCLOSED!
B-100 ($10 Value)
Wisdom Is The Principal Thing

Songs...

1. A Holy Place
2. Anything You Want
3. Everything Comes From You
4. Fill This Place With Your Presence
5. First Thing Every Morning
6. Holy Spirit, I Want To Hear You
7. Holy Spirit, Move Again
8. Holy Spirit, You Are Enough
9. I Don't Know What I Would Do Without You
10. I Let Go (Of Anything That Stops Me)
11. I'll Just Fall On You
12. I Love You, Holy Spirit
13. I'm Building My Life Around You
14. I'm Giving Myself To You
15. I'm In Love! I'm In Love!
16. I Need Water (Holy Spirit, You're My Well)
17. In The Secret Place

18. In Your Presence, I'm Always Changed
19. In Your Presence (Miracles Are Born)
20. I've Got To Live In Your Presence
21. I Want To Hear Your Voice
22. I Will Do Things Your Way
23. Just One Day At A Time
24. Meet Me In The Secret Place
25. More Than Ever Before
26. Nobody Else Does What You Do
27. No No Walls!
28. Nothing Else Matters Anymore (Since I've Been In The Presence Of You Lord)
29. Nowhere Else
30. Once Again You've Answered
31. Only A Fool Would Try (To Live Without You)
32. Take Me Now
33. Teach Me How To Please You

34. There's No Place I'd Rather Be
35. Thy Word Is All That Matters
36. When I Get In Your Presence
37. You're The Best Thing (That's Ever Happened To Me)
38. You Are Wonderful
39. You've Done It Once
40. You Keep Changing Me
41. You Satisfy

The Wisdom Center
6 Tapes / Only $30*
PAK007
Wisdom Is The Principal Thing

Add 10% For S/H

THE WISDOM CENTER
4051 Denton Highway • Fort Worth, TX 76117

1-817-759-BOOK
1-817-759-0300

You Will Love Our Website...!
TheWisdomCenter.tv

G

101 Wisdom Keys That Have Most Changed My Life.

The SCHOOL of WISDOM

SERIES 2

101 WISDOM KEYS THAT HAVE MOST CHANGED MY LIFE

MIKE MURDOCK

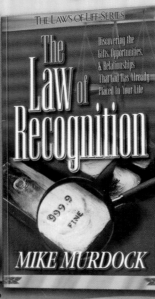

THE LAWS OF LIFE SERIES

The Law of Recognition

Discovering the Gifts, Opportunities, & Relationships That God Has Already Placed In Your Life

MIKE MURDOCK

TS-42

101 WISDOM KEYS THAT HAVE MOST CHANGED MY LIFE

DR. MIKE MURDOCK

School of Wisdom #2 Pak!

- ▶ What Attracts Others Toward You
- ▶ The Secret Of Multiplying Your Financial Blessings
- ▶ What Stops The Flow Of Your Faith
- ▶ Why Some Fail And Others Succeed
- ▶ How To Discern Your Life Assignment
- ▶ How To Create Currents Of Favor With Others
- ▶ How To Defeat Loneliness
- ▶ 47 Keys In Recognizing The Mate God Has Approved For You
- ▶ 14 Facts You Should Know About Your Gifts And Talents
- ▶ 17 Important Facts You Should Remember About Your Weakness
- ▶ And Much, Much More...

1

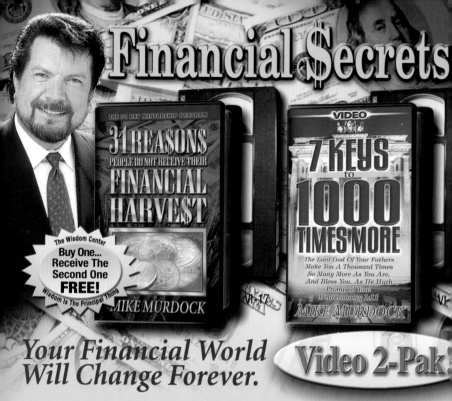

Financial $ecrets

THE 31 DAY MENTORSHIP PROGRAM

31 REASONS
PEOPLE DO NOT RECEIVE THEIR
FINANCIAL HARVE$T
MIKE MURDOCK

The Wisdom Center
Buy One...
Receive The
Second One
FREE!
Wisdom Is The Principal Thing

VIDEO

7 KEYS
to
1000
TIMES MORE
The Lord God Of Your Fathers
Make You A Thousand Times
So Many More As You Are,
And Bless You, As He Hath
Promised You!
Deuteronomy 1:11
MIKE MURDOCK

Your Financial World Will Change Forever.

Video 2-Pak!

▶ 8 Scriptural Reasons You Should Pursue Financial Prosperity

▶ The Secret Prayer Key You Need When Making A Financial Request To Go

▶ The Weapon Of Expectation And The 5 Miracles It Unlocks

▶ How To Discern Those Who Qualify To Receive Your Financial Assistance

▶ How To Predict The Miracle Moment God Will Schedule Your Financial Br through

▶ Habits Of Uncommon Achievers

▶ The Greatest Success Law I Ever Discovered

▶ How To Discern Your Place Of Assignment, The Only Place Financial Provision Is Guaranteed

▶ 3 Secret Keys In Solving Problems For Others

The Wisdom Center
Video 2-Pak!
Only $30 $60 Value
VIPAK-01
Wisdom Is The Principal Thing

Add 10% For S/H

J **THE WISDOM CENTER** **1-817-759-BOOK**
WISDOM CENTER 4051 Denton Highway • Fort Worth, TX 76117 **1-817-759-0300**

You Will Love Our Website...!
TheWisdomCenter.tv

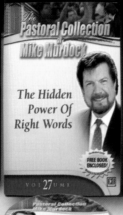

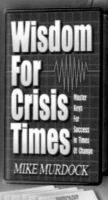

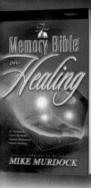

THE WISDOM BIBLE

Partnership Edition

Over 120 Wisdom Study Guides Included Such As:

- ▶ *10 Qualities Of Uncommon Achievers*
- ▶ *18 Facts You Should Know About The Anointing*
- ▶ *21 Facts To Help You Identify Those Assigned To You*
- ▶ *31 Facts You Should Know About Your Assignment*
- ▶ *8 Keys That Unlock Victory In Every Attack*
- ▶ *22 Defense Techniques To Remember During Seasons Of Personal Attack*
- ▶ *20 Wisdom Keys And Techniques To Remember During An Uncommon Battle*
- ▶ *11 Benefits You Can Expect From God*
- ▶ *31 Facts You Should Know About Favor*
- ▶ *The Covenant Of 58 Blessings*
- ▶ *7 Keys To Receiving Your Miracle*
- ▶ *16 Facts You Should Remember About Contentious People*
- ▶ *5 Facts Solomon Taught About Contracts*
- ▶ *7 Facts You Should Know About Conflict*
- ▶ *6 Steps That Can Unlock Your Self-Confidence*
- ▶ *And Much More!*

Your Partnership makes such a difference in The Wisdom Center Outreach Ministries. I wanted to place a Gift in your hand that could last a lifetime for you and your family...**The Wisdom Study Bible.**

40 Years of Personal Notes...this Partnership Edition Bible contains 160 pages of my Personal Study Notes...that could forever change your Bible Study of The Word of God. This **Partnership Edition...**is my personal **Gift of Appreciation** when you sow your Sponsorship Seed of $1,000 to help us complete The Prayer Center and TV Studio Complex. An Uncommon Seed Always Creates An Uncommon Harvest!

Mike

Thank you from my heart for your Seed of Obedience (Luke 6:38).

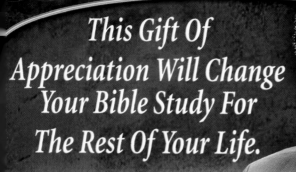

This Gift Of Appreciation Will Change Your Bible Study For The Rest Of Your Life.

The Wisdom Bible

THE WISDOM CENTER
4051 Denton Highway • Fort Worth, TX 76117

1-817-759-**BOOK**
1-817-759-0300

You Will Love Our Website...!
TheWisdomCenter.tv

0

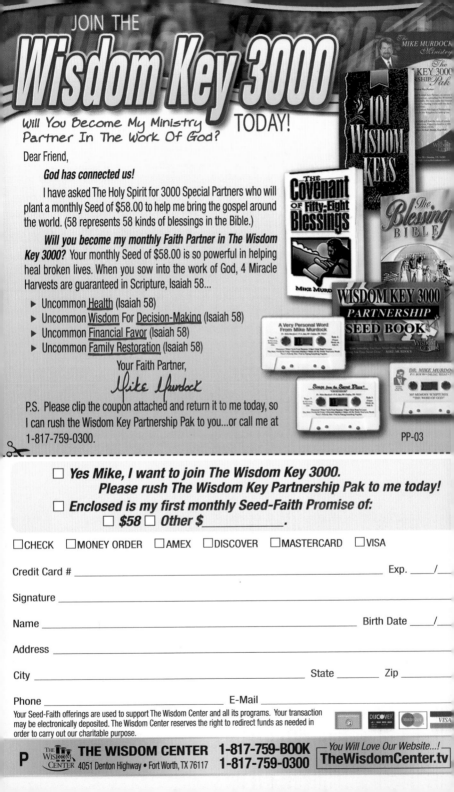